Restoration 1
Business Opportunity

As Featured in
12 Amazing Franchise Opportunities
— Second Edition —

Praise for the first edition of

12 Amazing Franchise Opportunities

"John Hayes's *12 Amazing Franchise Opportunities* provides crucial and critical information for those who aspire to fame and fortune in the wonderful world of franchising. He knows and expresses clearly and coherently- most- if not all- of the many nuances there are in franchising. This is a must read for those who are already franchisors and franchisees, but especially for those who aspire to become successful as either."

William B. Cherkasky, former President
International Franchise Association
Former Executive Director
U.S Senate Committee on Small Business

"Dr. Hayes has an amazing ability to uncomplicated the franchise buying process. He's able to provide invaluable insight in the entire selection and purchase process. Dr. Hayes provides a road map. Which simplifies what would otherwise be a difficult and confusing process."

Tom Portesy, President
MFV Expositions

"It was through my involvement with International Franchise Association that I came to know and respect John Hayes, author of this book. John has been a featured lecturer at many IFA events, both from the perspective of the franchisor and the franchisee. He is an acknowledged industry expert. I have listened to his advice and if you are thinking about investing I a franchise, you should, too."

Gary Goranson
Founder and former CEO of Tidy Car
Founder and owner of WorkEnders, Inc.
Coach and creator of www.HouseCleaningBiz101.com

"Dr. John Hayes is the world's leading authority on franchising. I know him as a franchisor, and when thinking about franchising our company he was my first call. You shouldn't make a franchise decision without reading everything Dr. Hayes has written on franchising.

J. Barry Watts, CEO
WealthCare Investment Advisors

"John's book is a must read for all prospective franchisees around the world. Most importantly, one must ask whether he/she has the personality, resources and commitment to work with the franchisor to achieve the desired success."

Albert Kong (CFE, CMC, Senior PMC)
Chairman/CEO
Asiawide Franchise Consultants Pte Ltd

"This is a fascinating book about a wide variety of franchising opportunities. If you want a road map to a new life in business, this is the book you must read!"

Mary Ellen Sheets, founder
Two Men & A Truck

"John Hayes is without question one of the world's foremost authorities on the subject of franchising and one of the most prolific and pertinent authors in this field. Congratulations on yet another informative and valuable resource book!"

Chris M. Levano, President
Quality Restaurant Consulting, Ltd.

"This one book should be read by every single franchise company and every single entrepreneur thinking of buying a franchise.... Everything this man writes or speaks I implement into my practice."

Mike Cheves, CEO
Hurricane Group, Inc.

"Coming from a thirty-year franchise veteran, 12 Amazing Franchise Opportunities for 2015, is one of the most profound and insightful publications I have ever read."

John L. Barry, President/CEO
Franchise Sales International

"John Hayes's 12 Amazing Franchise Opportunities 2015 serves as not only a primer for those interested in launching their own business, but also as an idea book that underscores the variety of opportunities that exist for wannabe business owners. A mobile dentistry repair unit? It's working and making money for franchisees. Hayes explains the concept of that and 11 other franchises that are waiting to come to your town. Spending a weekend with this book might just change your life."

Richard J. Farrell
Journalist/Columnist

"Excellent, and to the point book! John is the consummate franchise expert and teacher. If you're serious about becoming a franchise business owner, then use this book as your guidebook to the best franchising opportunity available today."

Bill Porter, Executive Vice President
Access Brand Management

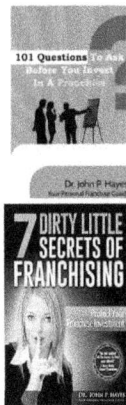

Other best-selling books by

<u>**John P. Hayes, Ph.D.**</u>

12 Amazing Franchise Opportunities Second Edition

Buy 'Hot' Franchises Without Getting Burned

101 Questions to Ask Before You Invest in a Franchise

Take the Fear Out of Franchising

7 Dirty Little Secrets of Franchising

Start Small Finish Big
(*15 key lessons* from the co-founder of Subway restaurants)

Mooney: Life of the World's Master Carver

Network Marketing for Dummies
(with Zig Ziglar)

James A. Michener: A Biography

You Can't Teach a Kid to Ride a Bike at a Seminar
(with David Sandler)

RESTORATION 1
Business Opportunity

Compiled by
Dr. John P. Hayes

BizComPress

Restoration 1 Business Opportunity

E-Book ISBN: 978-1-948851-03-9

Paperback ISBN: 978-1-948851-04-6

Copyright, 2018, John P. Hayes, Ph.D.

BizCom Press
1400 Preston Road, #305
Plano, TX 75093
www.BizComPress.com

Read this Disclaimer

CONTENTS
Restoration 1 Business Opportunity

Sponsored advertising content. Restoration 1 provided this chapter to tell its story.

Foreword

An Amazing Franchise: Restoration 1

Amazing...*causing great surprise or wonder; astonishing* according to the dictionary. But isn't franchising all about standards, consistency and predictable outcomes? It certainly is! Yet, the "amazing" part is how you can participate in a business model where you reap the reward for your efforts *and* you benefit from the collective efforts of the network, including the other franchisees, the vendor partners and the franchise concept owner.

On the planet today, there is no other model that can provide this type of leverage and synergy for anyone seeking the independence of business ownership. I have spent almost 30 years participating in the franchise sector, mostly as a franchisor, but also as a franchisee, consultant and educator, and there is no better time I've seen than now to foray into this entrepreneurial arena.

Dr. Hayes presents this Amazing Franchise concept worthy of your consideration. As you dive into Restoration 1, take your mind on a roller coaster ride of potential as you imagine yourself at the helm of this concept in your hometown. Ponder how you could embrace, enhance and expand this Amazing Franchise through your personal network, your social influence and your business acumen. Consider the value you could create partnering with Restoration 1 which will provide you with training, technology, resources and support along your journey. Relish in the knowledge that your efforts would be matched by the others in this Amazing Franchise to create a return beyond your capabilities alone. This is the magic of franchising and this Amazing Franchise!

Centuries ago, the Kings of old realized the power of the franchise model, granting villagers the "independence and freedom" to be a blacksmith, a farmer or a cobbler, providing needed services to their communities. The King granted them their "franchise" to pursue their passion and their trade, and to reap as much benefit as was possible, so long as they provided a "royalty to the King".

Today, Restoration 1 provides you the grant of independence and freedom to reap as much benefit as you can, operating as an independent business owner, so long as you return your share to provide support for the network. Yet, many will stay safely on their couches refusing to take that next important step of discovery which may well lead to the personal satisfaction they desire. Don't let this opportunity pass you by; embrace it and see where it leads.

For over a decade I have taught executives the franchise model through the Certificate in Franchise Management Program at Georgetown University's School of Continuing Studies in Washington, D.C. They come from all across the U.S. and around the world to gain a critical understanding of this most powerful of all business models, hoping to extract even a modicum of its potential to transform their concept into a globally recognized brand. Yet, none of them will succeed without highly motivated franchisees who provide the local attention to the brand needed to make it personal. The competitive advantage of the franchisee is their ability to connect with their community, navigate the pulse of the local economy and field the best team possible on the street. Every brand needs ambassadors to bring their concepts to life in the local community and every franchisor wants to engage with the highest quality individuals to represent their concepts as if it were truly their own.

As you look at Restoration 1 consider what you bring to the potential relationship: your personal talent, a strong connection to a local marketplace, hard-earned capital that deserves an above-market rate of return, and a commitment to contributing to the value of the brand to the good of the overall network. You should expect from this franchisor partner an equal commitment to continuous monitoring of the marketplace and modifications to the system as needed, the foresight to anticipate challenges and provide you with strong leadership to power through them, and a relentless focus on building brand value, the common denominator in the franchise equation.

The power of franchising has never been as strong as it is now, and it is a testament to the collective efforts of each participant in the network. It is critical that each participant in a franchise be willing to "give up their personal preference for the good of the network," and when that culture of collective effort pervades a brand, everyone associated with the brand benefits, including the customers served.

At the end of the day, the customers will decide the ultimate value of any business and any brand. And when the customer response is strong, the benefits to the network are amazing...higher pricing, stronger margins, exponential resale value. Take advantage of this unique opportunity to gain a glimpse inside Restoration 1 and take a journey of discovery that could well lead to the proverbial pot of gold. Be discerning, ask the difficult questions, and do your homework... franchising is no guarantee of success. But for those who persevere to find the right concept for their ability, the right fit for their market, and the right investment for their budget they may well join the ranks of millions that have gone before to a life of independence as a business owner without having to invent the business. And that is truly amazing!

— Dr. Ben Litalien, CFE

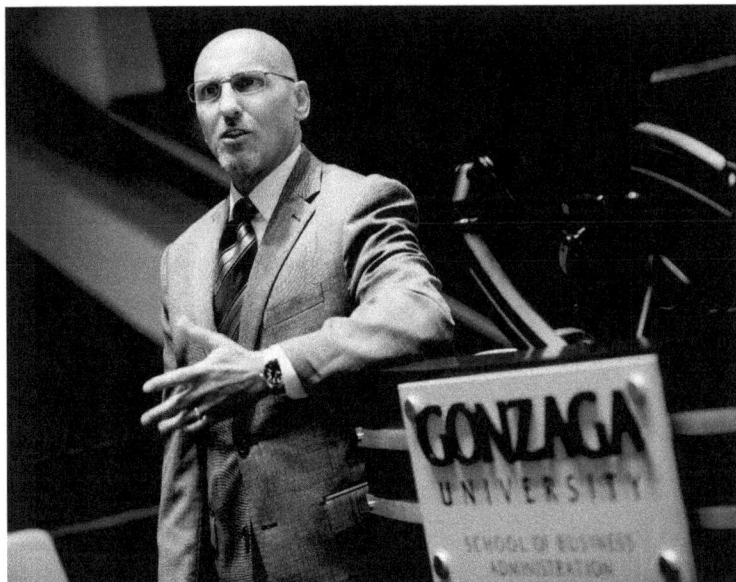

Dr. Ben Litalien is a professor in franchising for the University of Maryland University College and at Georgetown University's School of Continuing Studies. He has practiced in franchising for almost three decades, owning and operating franchises in the automotive, foodservice and hospitality sectors. He consults with a wide variety of firms on building franchise concepts including IKEA, ExxonMobil, The UPS Store and RE/MAX. He resides in Stafford County, Virginia with his wife of 32 years. They have three children and four grandsons. He enjoys spending time at their cabin in West Virginia, fly-fishing whenever possible. Reach Dr. Litalien via email or visit his website at

FranchiseWell.com.

Introduction

If you already know about franchising and you think it's an amazing concept, you may want to skip the Introduction and head directly into the chapter about Restoration 1. But if you're curious about why I think franchising is amazing, and you want to know more about what's in this book, please continue reading.

The first time a franchisor explained to me how franchising works, I thought the concept was amazing. After building a successful business, a franchisor offers (of course, for a fee) to teach others how to operate the same business in a different location or market. Amazing…and here's why.

Got an Amazing Idea?

Most people can't come up with a good business idea, let alone know how to build a prototype and successfully open the doors to paying customers. Most people are going to trip up over where to locate the business, or how to negotiate with suppliers, or how to market and advertise the business, or how to charge for products or services, or how to keep customers coming back time after time, or all of that and more.

In other words, most people who start a business are going to fail, and they do. Every year would-be business owners lose billions of dollars in America alone, all because they didn't know what successful franchisors know.

The Secret is in the System

You'll notice that I said "successful franchisors" because not everyone who becomes a franchisor succeeds. But successful franchisors, those who invest the time and the money—especially the money—to build profitable and satisfying businesses also develop a series of systems that they can transfer and teach to other people: franchisees. Everything that successful franchisors know becomes part of a

14

system. And it's the system that franchisees rely on to replicate the franchisor's success.

How does McDonald's eliminate the guesswork about where to open a new unit? That knowledge is part of McDonald's site selection system.

How does a McDonald's franchisee know how many hamburger rolls to purchase on any given day, and how many employees to schedule to operate the business during an eight-hour shift? The answers are part of McDonald's operating system.

In fact, you can't ask a question that McDonald's, the franchisor, can't answer about how to operate a successful McDonald's restaurant. And now, just imagine, McDonald's is willing to share all of its knowledge with you, or any qualified prospect, to become a franchisee anywhere in the world. Tell me that's not amazing!

You Can Minimize the Risk

What's more amazing, and this is what I thought about the first time a franchisor explained franchising to me, is that I do not have to come up with a good business idea, go into debt to develop the idea in the hopes that it would become a profitable and satisfying business, and then fail.

I don't have to take that risk because there are at least 3,800 different franchise opportunities in North America alone. It's easier to find a business concept that I like, and then pay the franchisor to teach me how to operate the business successfully in a new location. Or, I can buy an existing franchise business and bypass the more treacherous start-up years.

I didn't come from a business-minded family, so I knew very little about how to develop and operate a business. And yet, I wanted to own a business because I knew that working for someone else wasn't going to fulfill my life-long expectations. I was never going to make enough money working for someone else, and I'm not a 9-to-5 type of employee.

But until I learned about franchising, I didn't think I could ever own a business. I've since owned several franchises, I've been the CEO of a major franchisor organization, and I've devoted a career to advising franchisors and franchisees,

15

writing about franchising, and teaching people how to take advantage of this amazing concept.

Franchising is an Equalizer

Through the years I've become acquainted with countless people internationally who told me they didn't think they had a chance to own a business because of their circumstances. Some of these people had great ideas for new businesses, but most of them did not have the money to start a business, and many of them did not have a formal education. In fact, several never graduated from high school. No one claimed to know how to build a business.

But once these people discovered franchising, most of their doubts and limitations disappeared over time, and they built profitable and satisfying businesses, and in some cases, financial empires.

It's important to know, as successful franchisors and franchisees will tell you, that while franchising levels the playing field so that most everyone can succeed in business, it doesn't suddenly make everything all right. It makes everything possible, at least in terms of developing a successful business, but it doesn't remove all the risks or limitations, and it surely doesn't do the work for you. Many people are fond of saying that franchising is "turnkey," and unfortunately that leads some people to believe that all they have to do is get the key, turn it, and voila!, success. But it's not *that* amazing!

Franchising isn't a miraculous solution. I don't know any lazy or uninformed people who have succeeded in franchising. Conversely, of the successful franchisors and franchisees I know, none is a genius. Most are simply hard-working, curious, ambitious people. Some earned college degrees; others did not. Some had family money; most did not. Many struggled before they succeeded, and some failed and started again, but none gave up.

Other than franchising as a common bond, successful franchisors and franchisees also share the ability to be led. Obviously, franchisees need to learn how to be successful in business—that's the purpose of the franchisor's system—but franchisors are not infinitely wise; the best of them recognize that they need to be taught and guided, too, and they invest time and money in their continuing

16

educations. Anyone who isn't willing to be led to greater accomplishments isn't cut out for franchising, as amazing as it may be.

But is Franchising for You?

Even if you agree with me that franchising is amazing, you ultimately have to decide if franchising is for you. You may already have decided that it is and that's why you're reading this book, or you may still be searching for answers even while you're searching for an amazing franchise opportunity. Either way, this book can help you make the decision. Because even though the book is devoted to telling you about 12 amazing franchise opportunities, I've also included additional information that will help you not only decide if franchising is for you, but if it is, what type of franchise is best for you.

Here's What's in the Book

The book includes important information about how to buy a franchise opportunity, sharing step-by-step instructions for making a good buying decision, including many of the questions you should ask. Check out "17 Steps to Successfully Buying a Franchise" and "How to Investigate Before You Invest in a Franchise." If you will need money to buy a franchise, I've covered that for you, too. You'll want to read "Funding Your Franchise Acquisition: Where Do You Get the Money?"

If you're not an American citizen, but you want to use your investment in a franchise or in franchising to move to America under the EB-5 Foreign Investor Program, you'll want to read "Use Franchising to Get Your U.S. Green Card."

Are you a Good Fit for Franchising?

Perhaps the most important chapter—the one you should read first—is "Match Your Personality to the Appropriate Franchise Opportunities." I can't say it often enough: As amazing as it is as a business development methodology, franchising is not for everyone. You can try to force a round peg into a square hole, but you know that's not going to work successfully. All that's going to do is create frustration and possibly a huge financial loss. So why not verify your compatibility with franchising before investing your money? It's easy to do (visit www.howtobuyafranchise.com/disc), it's free, and you'll find out how in this book.

Restoration 1 provided the chapter that describes its amazing franchise opportunity. Prior to that chapter, I include information about why I believe Restoration 1 is an amazing opportunity.

Franchising Caters to Your Desires

Here's another amazing fact about franchising. There's something for (almost) everyone!

- You want to work from home? You can.
- You want to work from a truck? You can.
- You want to work in a store at the mall or a strip center? You can.
- You want to provide a service instead of selling a product? You can.
- You want to own multiple units of the same franchise brand? You can.
- You want to own multiple franchise brands? You can.
- You want to own a territory in which you sell the franchises and then train and support the franchisees while also owning your own unit? You can.
- You want to live the life of an expat building an international franchise empire? You can.

The opportunities are endless. If franchising makes sense for you—and it does not for everyone—then it's a matter of finding the right opportunity. There's a good chance Restoration 1 is the right opportunity for you. If it is, your next step is to request information from the franchisor.

For now, the only thing left to do is continue reading!

— Dr. John P. Hayes
April 2018

Is Franchising for You?

One of the most important lessons that I've learned through the years is that many of the people who could be successful franchisees fail as franchisees simply because they bought the wrong franchise.

Granted, some people fail because they are not cut out for franchising, and regardless of which franchise they buy, or how much money they invest, they are destined to fail. I can't say this often enough: Franchising is not for everyone!

It's easy to discover if franchising is for you, so I hope you'll take the time to find out. If it is for you, it's also easy to discover the type of franchise that's best suited for you.

Sadly, many people miss this information and that's why I'm placing this chapter at the front of this book. I not only don't want you to miss it, but I don't think you should pursue any franchise opportunity until you know if you're a good fit for franchising. Why invest the time and the money? Why put yourself at risk?

The last thing you need—the last thing franchising needs—is a business failure. Many franchisee failures, and many of the situations that result in disgruntled franchisor/franchisee relationships (which ultimately tarnish franchising's reputation), could be avoided if people just paid attention to the information in this chapter.

Failed Franchisees Missed this Lesson

This is one of the most important lessons that you, as a prospective franchisee, can learn about franchising. Do yourself the favor that many franchisees before you did not do—learn this lesson and follow it!

Every franchisor should pay attention to this lesson, too, and implement the protective steps that will help their franchisees succeed. But there's another pertinent truth that you should know about franchising: Franchisors are not created equal! Some care more about selling franchises than they care about the success and satisfaction of franchisees.

My Personal Experience with Profiling

My personal story explains why I'm adamant about franchise profiling. The founder of the franchise company, HomeVestors of America, Inc., where I eventually served as president and CEO, died unexpectedly. Ken D'Angelo was a magnificent person, and one of the most conscientious franchisors, and unfortunately, he died at a time when his company was moving from a start-up to a professionally run organization. He had developed a time-tested operating system, the only one of its kind that taught people from all walks of life how to buy and sell real estate for a profit. I was not only an adviser to Ken, but I served on his Board of Directors. I also owned a HomeVestors franchise, which was operated by my partner.

To Ken, investing in real estate was akin to crossing a busy highway—you had to study the situation, calculate the variables, know where to look and what to look for, and ultimately know when to step out and seize the moment. And to Ken, who had no formal education beyond high school, anyone could follow his amazing system and succeed as a real estate investor. And many people did (especially while sub-prime lending existed).

When I succeeded Ken at his request in 2004, HomeVestors had some 250 franchisees buying almost 10,000 houses a year in 30-some states. The company was essentially a marketing machine for real estate investors. Our "We Buy Ugly Houses" billboard campaigns, along with other advertising, generated upwards of 250,000 leads every year for our franchisees!

Every year, HomeVestors organized an annual meeting where Ken and others provided insights and updates about real estate investing, as well as training, networking, and awards. Lots of awards.

Real estate investors come with big egos—most franchisees come with big egos—and a good way to keep them happy and engaged in your business is to publicly reward them for their achievements. Ken was giving his top-performing franchisees Ford F-150 pickup trucks, as well as trophies and cash.

But now here's the odd twist: The top franchisees weren't necessarily getting the best awards.

Identifying Top Franchisees

Who's a top franchisee? That's no different than asking any business owner: Who's your best customer? But most business owners, including franchisors and franchisees, can't answer that question accurately, so it's not surprising that Ken couldn't, either. In any business, the best customer is the one who comes back time after time and pays you (the business owner) the most money without disrupting your business.

When Ken decided to reward franchisees, he looked at several qualifiers, but essentially, he rewarded those who bought the most houses in a year's time. Made sense to me, but for some reason one day after I was appointed president I asked our financial folks to provide me with a list of franchisees ranked by royalty value. In other words, I said, show me the franchisees in ranked order with the one who paid us the most money in royalties at #1 on the list, and the one who paid us the least money in royalties at #250 (or whatever number was last place) on the list.

"Do We Know these Franchisees?"

When I got the list, I said to my leadership team: Who are these people at the top of the list?

They were not the franchisees we had been awarding year after year. Some were, but most were not. In fact, I had never met some of the franchisees, and in the four years that I had worked closely with Ken, he never mentioned them to me, and I don't think he ever visited them in their markets (and we visited many franchisees every year).

Turns out the top franchisees may also be those you rarely hear from…they do not complain, they do not make requests, they do not (necessarily) want to speak at your meetings and conventions, they do not demand that you come and visit them…they just work the system and, well, make money!

The Top Franchisee Report, as I started referring to that list, triggered a gold mine of information and provided tremendous insight for how we should spend our time as a franchisor. For example, our operations folks spent an inordinate amount of time helping many of the lower-rung franchisees who never seemed to be able to work our system.

We thought that if we spent more time (and money) coaching, training, and encouraging these franchisees, they might eventually catch on and perform better…but there was little evidence of that.

The fact was, the best way to help some of those bottom-rung franchisees was to find a buyer for their franchise and let them move on to another occupation. They were simply not fit for our business, and we should not have sold them a franchise.

"What's Different about These Franchisees?"

After I got over my initial surprise about the contents of the list, I asked another question: Why these franchisees?

Now I wanted to know why the top 25 franchisees were the top 25 franchisees. Why them, and not the bottom 25? Obviously the top 25 paid us the most money. But what were they doing that the bottom 25 were not doing? Or, why were the top 25 so much more capable than the bottom 25?

Best of all, I asked: What can we do to make sure we only award future franchises to people who will show up in the top 25, or help expand the top 25 to the top 50?

There were numerous answers to that question, but one of the most pertinent was: Assess their personalities to make sure they're a fit for our business. Actually, Ken had already been doing that, but now it was time to pay more attention to the results.

We had to be sure we were awarding franchises to people who were a good fit for our business.

Obviously, we hadn't done the best job of that in the past, but now we knew how to improve. In doing so, we'd also improve franchisee morale and satisfaction. And it all worked well, until the Great Recession, but that's an entirely different story.

How to Use Your Assessment

You do not need a franchisor to tell you whether or not you're a good fit for franchising (you can find that out on your own and I'll show you how in a moment), but it would be a huge benefit if a franchisor told you whether or not you were a good fit for their business.

Unfortunately, many (maybe most) franchisors can't do that because (a) they don't know or think it's important, (b) they don't know how, (c) they think it would slow down their sales, and/or (d) they've never profiled their franchisees so they don't know who's best-suited for their business. If I were you, before investing in any franchise, I would insist on getting more of this "intelligence" from a franchisor. Some—but not enough—franchisors use personality assessment tools, and I would favor them.

You can quickly get an assessment of your personality by using the DiSC® assessment at www.howtobuyafranchise.com/disc. DiSC measures your behavioral differences or patterns and is at least a preliminary—and free—assessment of your personality and your compatibility with franchising.

The DiSC Personality Profile is not franchise specific, but it provides interesting insights about an individual's strengths characterized in terms of Dominance, Influence, Steadiness, and Compliance.

A Dominant personality, for example, might do well in a business that depends on the franchisee to generate sales; a Compliant personality probably would not succeed in such a business. However, a Compliant personality might do well in a service business that interacts closely with customers, while a Dominant personality might not succeed in such a business.

The Influencer and Steady personalities are likely to excel in businesses that depend on teamwork. Unlike the Dominant and Competent personalities, the I and S personalities like working with other people. However, these personalities require clear and specific operating systems, and strong franchisor support, to succeed.

Many franchisors use DiSC or some form of it, and as a result they can tell you the behaviors that are most successful (and those that are least successful) in their business. If your behaviors differ from those of the most successful franchisees, you're probably not going to become a profitable and satisfied franchisee in that business. Now wouldn't you really like to know that before investing your money? Shouldn't a franchisor want to know that, too?

Before you go any further in your pursuit of franchising, take the time to assess your personality. It's a good protective measure. It takes about ten minutes to complete the DiSC assessment: (www.howtobuyafranchise.com/disc).

Give Yourself an Edge

Franchise companies do not need to rely on personality profiling to be amazing, but amazing franchisors are always interested in a franchise candidate's profiling results and how the results relate to their business. So share your results and ask the franchisors if your behavioral patterns will help you succeed in their business.

Some franchisors, as well as franchise brokers, will ask you to complete their preferred, and sometimes proprietary, assessment, and you should be eager to do so.

Using personality assessments and matching the results to appropriate franchise opportunities levels the playing field and ultimately helps you succeed in franchising. Don't go any further until you identify your personality profile!

— Dr. John P. Hayes
West Palm Beach, Florida

Restoration 1
WATER DAMAGE EXPERTS

If you like being on top, then you'll like being a part of the Restoration 1 franchise network. In 2017 alone, *Entrepreneur* magazine ranked the franchise opportunity on the Franchise 500 list, the Fastest-Growing Franchises list, the Top Franchises Under $100K list, and the Top Franchises For Veterans list. These accolades help underscore why the network has grown from eighteen locations to more than 175 in the last couple of years.

Restoration 1 franchisees get the chance to be a hero every time they go to work because when customers call, they are experiencing an emergency, and Restoration 1 franchisees get to save the day. How many franchisees can say that?

The Restoration 1 franchise network includes former Wall Street employees, corporate executives, military veterans, retirees pursuing their second career, new college graduates, and even the brand's first female franchise owner. The typical qualities they all share include the desire to be the boss, their attraction to realizing a strong return on their investment, their appreciation of being a part of a growing national brand, and the forward-thinking of an exit strategy when they are ready to leave the business.

Restoration 1 franchisees reap the rewards of national vendor relationships, access to the best suppliers and services, a professional online presence, the design of professionally branded trucks and uniforms, a strong peer network, an experienced support team at corporate headquarters, and an industry with built-in demand. And, most of all, the Restoration 1 network epitomizes how dirty jobs pay well.

If you'd appreciate an amazing business in the $60 billion restoration industry, continue reading to learn more about Restoration 1.

— Dr. John P. Hayes, CFE

Finding Franchise Success in the $60 Billion Restoration Industry

Timing is everything, as the saying goes. Just ask Beth Hendriks, of Raleigh, North Carolina.

When a heavy storm sent a tree crashing through the roof of one of her rental properties, Hendriks managed the repairs to her rental home by herself. In the process, she encountered the frustrating experience and countless headaches of working with contract workers she hired to handle the repairs. She was able to complete the restoration project on her own, but she knew there had to be a better, more efficient way to do the job.

The disaster led Hendriks to a future in one of the fastest-growing franchise opportunities: Restoration 1. It was only a matter of time before she started providing a critical service to others in her community.

The timing was perfect because when the disaster struck, Hendriks also happened to be researching various franchise opportunities for a future investment. After years as a C-wing executive with a nice parachute to put toward a new venture, she came upon Restoration 1. And, like other corporate evacuees looking to transition from a corner office to be the boss in another lucrative field, she dove straight into the restoration industry.

"Going through the restoration process from a customer's point of view really opened my eyes to what customers want and need from a restoration company," Hendriks said. "When I found Restoration 1, they were already connecting all those dots, and I knew this was a business where I could excel."

Her business savvy zeroed in on a great company with superior customer service that would be perfect for her in a field that has an ongoing demand. Hendriks was ready to offer others a solution without all the headaches.

Some 14,000 people in the U.S. experience a water damage emergency at home or work each day. The annual cost to insurance companies from water and mold tops $2.5 billion each year. And a whopping 37 percent of homeowners claim to have suffered losses from water damage.

As CEO, franchise veteran Gary Findley has Restoration 1 on a strong growth path.

Rapid, Yet Steady Growth

Founded in 2008, Restoration 1 is an award-winning organization that specializes in fire, water, and mold remediation services. Franchisees also provide emergency and storm-damage services, sewage system cleanup and more. With locations across more than half the U.S. and a rapid yet steady pace of expansion, Restoration 1 has become one of the fastest-growing and most-trusted restoration franchises in America.

In addition, franchisees point to four key elements about the business that get them up and running quickly: recession resistant, low overhead, low investment level, and no brick-and-mortar location to get started.

Of course, that doesn't mean just anyone can do the work. As disaster restoration experts, Restoration 1 franchisees are professionally trained to step in and handle emergencies, no matter how big or small, at a moment's notice. Every second counts when dealing with property damage, so Restoration 1 franchisees are committed to helping customers preserve their property, including keepsakes inside their home or business, and getting the property owners back to their normal day-to-day as quickly as possible.

Getting Down and Dirty

Putting the "restore" into restoration is where customers' hang their hopes and expectations. To do that, Restoration 1 franchisees are certified by the Institute of Inspection and Indoor Air Quality Association (IAQA), and have a Cleaning and Restoration Certification (IICRC).

These certifications help give property owners confidence that their restoration project is being handled by fully trained professionals.

Restoration 1 franchisees are heroes when tragedy strikes. While it can be a dirty business, it's also a billion-dollar industry that gives Restoration 1 franchisees an incredible chance to shine.

As another popular saying goes, things will get worse before they get better. That's entirely true when a typical day on the job can include tearing out drywall, pulling up carpet, and removing cabinets to get to affected areas that need attention. But when Restoration 1 delivers on the brand promise and a 100 percent satisfaction guarantee, nothing compares to the peace of mind, appreciation, and loyalty of a happy customer whose life can get back to normal.

So, who exactly are those "typical helpers"? These award-winning franchisees are part of one of the fastest-growing franchises in North America and come from all walks of life.

When Beth Hendriks signed her franchise agreement in May 2017 to open multiple locations in the Raleigh, North Carolina area, she became Restoration 1's first female franchisee.

No stranger to breaking glass ceilings, she previously spent 27 years in the tech industry as one of a limited number of female executives with a computer science background. It was this background that also made her appreciate the technology infrastructure and support built into Restoration 1's franchise model, which helps her run the business.

This mom of six is clearly not intimidated by a male-dominated field. Enthusiastic and well-suited to take the restoration industry by storm, she is building a successful franchise business focused on giving her customers the experience she would have appreciated when restoring her own property.

Franchisees are not required to operate a brick-and-mortar location to get their business running, reducing the initial investment needed.

Age Doesn't Determine Success

Just like gender, age is no barrier to becoming a Restoration 1 franchisee. Today, across a growing network of franchisees, the organization is attracting retirees looking for a new project, corporate refugees escaping the trappings of Corporate America, and even recent college graduates making the transition from student to business owner.

Recent graduates Francisco Burciaga and Alfonso Masso literally crossed the stage to receive their college diplomas and moved straight into a new franchise territory, opening their own business together.

Meeting as sophomores at Baylor University, Burciaga and Masso made their way through the entrepreneurship curriculum in the school of business and soon realized that franchising was a perfect fit and an ideal avenue to help them achieve their entrepreneurial dreams.

"Graduation came around and you start asking yourself, 'What's going to pay the bills now?'" said Burciaga. "We definitely didn't want to give up on entrepreneurial dreams, but at the same time, a grassroots startup idea fresh out of college was incredibly risky."

What started as a typical friendship between former college roommates quickly transformed into a business partnership. Burciaga and Masso got advice from other franchisees on securing financing and were signing papers to become Restoration 1 franchise owners within a week of their college graduation.

"They all said just walk into a local credit union, tell them your story, tell them the story about Restoration 1. It was nice to be able to go in and shake the hand of the person approving the loan," said Burciaga. "It definitely helped to be a franchisee and to come in with some history—this is the CEO, this is what the average franchisee makes."

They jumped head first into training and completing their certifications. Soaking up all the experience and information they could during training, the pair set up shop by purchasing their first van. In no time, they were answering their first business call – a water-damage and mold-removal job.

Today, they are operating a thriving franchise in Austin, Texas, and celebrated their first business anniversary in the fall of 2017.

From Combat Boots to Work Boots

Retired military veterans also find a good fit with Restoration 1.

After spending 13 years in the military, Joey Buchino knew one thing for certain – he DID NOT want to work for anyone when he returned to civilian life. Buchino thought his military training in the U.S. Army had perfectly primed him for franchise ownership. Thanks to Uncle Sam and the discipline and leadership skills needed to serve in the Armed Forces, Joey learned the value of following a system. He found a similar system to follow in the business world with Restoration

1. As a participant in the VetFran program, Restoration 1 is one of the respected franchise organizations that offers discounts to veterans who want to purchase a franchise.

"I knew I wanted to be my own boss," said Buchino, who owns a franchise in Parkland, Florida. "I knew nothing about owning or running a business. So, I went into franchising with Restoration 1 because I knew that it would shorten my learning curve when it came to business."

While he didn't have any formal experience owning or running a business, the Restoration 1 franchise has proven to be a smooth transition as he traded in combat boots for work boots and began to get down and dirty in his own business.

While he may have traded in one uniform for another, Buchino wakes up every day and finds himself using skills he learned in the Army to lead his Restoration 1 teams on important and time-sensitive missions.

Recession-proof Opportunity

What attracts so many franchisees from so many different walks of life to the Restoration 1 franchise network? Perhaps the biggest attraction is the opportunity to own a business in a $60 billion industry that is not only here to stay, but is increasingly in demand. Because disaster can — and often does — strike at any time, the restoration industry has proven to be recession-proof. Natural and man-made disasters don't take days off, which means restoration professionals experience a constant need for their services.

Because natural and man-made disasters never take time off, the restoration industry has proven to be recession-proof.

Another reason the demand for restoration services is expected to grow is because the majority of Americans are living in older homes, where mold and water damage has become an increasing problem.

The health consequences associated with mold, smoke, and fire damage are well known and must be addressed quickly and professionally.

An Affordable Opportunity, a Winning Team

One attractive feature of the Restoration 1 opportunity is that franchisees are not required to operate a brick-and-mortar location to get their business running. As a result, they benefit from low overhead startup costs. Restoration 1 franchisees can operate their business out of a van as they build clientele and revenue. They are able to add a physical location when they are ready and financially stable. As a result, Restoration 1 has become one of the fastest-growing and most-trusted restoration franchises in the country.

Keeping the brand on the fast track for growth is CEO Gary Findley, a veteran in the franchise industry with over 25 years of experience. He previously helped two other franchise chains grow to over 9,500 locations worldwide.

"I credit our phenomenal franchise sales team and a franchise opportunity that has attracted the most incredible prospects in my entire career of franchising," Findley said. "From Wall Street executives and corporate evacuees, to military veterans and successful entrepreneurs, we have the most qualified leaders joining our network."

Findley is committed to growing the Restoration 1 franchise brand, and his immediate goals include expanding to more than 500 locations nationwide as well as expanding internationally with an immediate focus on the Canadian and UK markets.

Helping to fuel the brand's growth is the recognition Restoration 1 receives on a local and national level. *Entrepreneur* magazine named Restoration 1 one of the fastest-growing franchises in its Fastest-Growing Franchise List in 2017 and catapulted the company from #396 to #96 on the Franchise 500 list based on its rapid success.

But it's not only the media paying attention. Restoration 1 customers from across the country are passionate about sharing positive experiences with friends, family, and social networks. Making a lasting impression on customers through excellent customer service in a time of need has helped spread the word and share the brand with new customers and potential franchisees.

Endless Opportunities on the Horizon

Like all successful franchise chains, however, Restoration 1 is not content to rest on its laurels. In 2017, the franchise introduced a content cleaning program. This gives franchisees an additional, optional business opportunity for franchisees who want to provide a total restoration solution for customers experiencing property damage or loss by also helping them with the contents within their property.

"The content cleaning program is an exciting opportunity for us as a brand and a great way for our franchisees to take on an additional revenue stream within their existing business," said Findley. "We continually look for ways to offer added value to our franchisees, and this is one example of going that extra step that not only delivers for our franchisees but also for their customers."

Additionally, Restoration 1's acquisition of bluefrog Plumbing + Drain® in 2017 offers further diversity and growth opportunities. Existing Restoration 1 franchisees can pair their restoration business with a plumbing franchise, providing a convenient one-stop shop for customers, further helping to ease and simplify their restoration experience.

"Our success continues to grow, and so do the communities that we serve to rescue customers from unthinkable disasters," said Findley.

More Information

Looking to get down and dirty with a Restoration 1 business of your own? Restoration 1 is looking for active and enthusiastic entrepreneurs. There are plenty of attractive and high-profile markets still available for growth. For more information, visit www.restoration1franchise.com or call **(888) 912-6450**.

17 Steps to Successfully Buying a Franchise

Everything is possible with a system!

Outstanding achievements are the result of someone following a system. With the right systems, you can succeed at almost anything. What is it that you want? There's a system to help you get it.

You want to successfully buy a franchise? It won't surprise you, I don't think, to discover that there's a system for doing so. And here it is: "17 Steps to Successfully Buying a Franchise." If you follow these guidelines, you're taking all the right steps to explore franchising, to consider the pros and cons of franchising, and, if franchising makes sense for you, to ultimately find a franchise opportunity worthy of your investment.

Even though I cannot guarantee your success as a franchisee—no one can because there are so many variables at play—if you complete these seventeen steps, you can eventually sign your name to a franchise agreement with the confidence that you've done everything possible to ensure your own success as a franchisee. Of course, you must follow the system and complete each step with integrity.

Based on that understanding, here are the 17 steps to successfully buying a franchise:

1.) Educate Yourself

As you prepare to buy a franchise, spend time reading (or viewing informational videos) to make sure you understand what franchising is all about. You can also get good information at franchise conferences and through franchise advisers. One way or another, get familiar with the fundamentals of franchising.

Questions you should ask:

- Why is franchising so successful?
- What are the main reasons for franchise failure?
- How can I be sure that a franchisor is legitimate?

2.) Why Franchising Exists

Of all the points that you need to understand about franchising, the most important may be this: Franchising is a system of distribution. Franchising is a means for marketing and selling products and services. Don't get caught up in any of the hype about franchising. Yes, of course, it's a way for you to own your own business, and it may be the safest way to do so, and it may be your ticket to financial independence, but do not overlook the fundamental purpose of franchising: It's to sell stuff!

Questions you should ask:

- Am I excited about distributing the franchisor's products and services?
- Do I see myself operating this system for five, ten, or more years
- How can I be sure that the franchisor's system will work in my territory?

3.) Are You a Good Fit for Franchising?

Be absolutely sure that franchising makes sense for you. Franchisors are not interested in selling franchises to the wrong prospects or investors. You should be equally as protective of yourself. Ask the question: Is franchising for me? Keep in mind that it's not for everyone. If it's not for you, don't force it. Read the chapter, "Match Your Personality to the Appropriate Franchise Opportunities" and complete the free DiSC assessment at www.howtobuyafranchise.com/disc.

Questions you should ask:

- What qualifies me to be a franchisee?
- Why do I want to be a franchisee?
- What type of franchise will make the most sense for me?

4.) Know Your Role as a Franchisee

Understand that the franchisor creates the system and the franchisees follow the system. Good franchisors know what needs to be done day to day, month to month, to succeed in the business. And that's what they'll expect you to do. Everything you're required to do is part of the system…so you must be willing to follow it, even if you don't always agree with it. Otherwise the franchisor can take away your franchise. The franchise agreement mandates that you follow the franchisor's system.

Questions you should ask:

- How can I learn more about the franchisor's system?
- What aspects of the system may or may not be of interest to me?
- Do existing franchisees endorse the franchisor's system?

5.) You're Buying a License

By legal definition, a franchise is a license. A franchisor licenses a franchisee to operate a specific business in a specific manner at a specific location (or in a specific region) for a specific period of time. The license can be renewed and either party also can terminate it. Be sure you understand those details before you invest.

Furthermore, the franchisor retains ownership of (almost) everything! The franchisor's intellectual property, training materials, marketing methodologies, sales processes, possibly even phone numbers and clients, always remain the property of the franchisor, and not the franchisee. These details will be explained in the Franchise Disclosure Document.

Questions you should ask:

- What are the specific terms of the franchise agreement?
- Do I get a protected territory? (You may not want a protected territory and you do not necessarily need one, depending on the franchise.)
- What if I decide I want to sell the franchise; how do I do that?

6.) The Franchise Work Environment

Think about the franchise work environment. Most franchisors require franchisees to be owners/operators. In other words, you can't be an absentee owner. Some franchisors expect franchisees to work from home, or a small office. Other franchisors require franchisees to work from a retail shop at a strip center or a mall. Other franchisors require franchisees to work from a van or another type of vehicle. In some cases, franchisees work alone; in other cases, franchisees manage employees. Once you know which work environment makes sense for you, pursue franchise opportunities that support your preferences.

Questions you should ask:

- Do I want to manage people?
- Am I comfortable working alone, from my home or a small office
- If I prefer one work environment but the franchise companies of my choice require a different work environment, can I adjust?

7.) Did You Know They Franchised That?

There are at least seventy-five primary industries that use franchising as their method of distribution. When people explore franchising, they're often surprised by the industries that use franchising as a methodology and by the vast array of franchise opportunities available. Some realize, for the first time, that franchising isn't just fast food! By reading this book, you'll discover franchises that provide cleaning, restoration, training, painting, recruitment, business services, and pet services, to name just several. What's important is to find the industry and the opportunity—or opportunities—that make sense for you.

Questions you should ask:

- Which industries interest me the most?
- Which industries can I afford?
- Which industries provide me with the best opportunities?

8.) Look for the Right Opportunity

No one knows exactly how many franchise opportunities exist, but there are three thousand to four thousand opportunities in North America alone. Many of these opportunities are local or regional, and some of the companies are sold out, so they're not offering franchises except internationally. Some industries include a dozen or more franchise companies offering similar and competitive franchise opportunities, while other industries may only include a handful of franchise opportunities.

Of course, these numbers are of little consequence considering that you're looking for just one franchise: The one that's best for you. You will find these opportunities by reading books and articles, attending expos, and by being observant: What's being franchised today that interests you?

Questions you should ask:

- How much money can I invest in a franchise? The answer may dictate the industries that you should explore.
- How do I want to spend the next five, ten, or more years of my life in business?
- When it comes to "selling stuff," what excites me?

9.) Information is Free; Ask for It!

When you find a company that interests you, ask for information. It's free, and it comes without any strings attached. Remember this: A U.S.-based franchisor must provide U.S. citizens with a disclosure document at least two weeks before selling a franchise. The clock doesn't begin to tick until you acknowledge receiving the disclosure document. I want to emphasize the document is free.

However, franchisors will not give you the disclosure document until they've had an opportunity to speak with you and know that you are qualified to invest in their business. You can expect the franchisor (via online entry or an interview with a representative) to ask you for your personal information, including your email address, phone number, the time frame in which you plan to buy a franchise, and an estimate of how much money you intend to invest in a business. You also may be asked for specific financial information. By the way, it's a mistake to provide misleading information—once you're found out, do you think the franchisor will trust you?

Questions you should ask:

- Are you planning to open franchises in my territory of choice?
- How much is the investment in your franchise?
- What makes your franchise business unique and amazing?

10.) Carefully Read the Information

Invest time to carefully read the preliminary information provided by the franchisor. Make sure you not only can see yourself as a franchisee in this concept, but that you at least preliminarily understand what you'll be expected to do as a franchisee. The information the franchisor provides may not be specific, but the information in the franchisor's disclosure document must be specific. If you like the initial information you get from a franchisor, then it's time to ask for the disclosure document.

Questions you should ask:

- If I were to invest in this franchise, what else would I need to know?
- Is this a business that makes sense for my location, or territory?
- Where's this business headed in the next five to ten years?

11.) Attend the Franchisor's Discovery Day

Visit the franchisor. Almost every franchisor sponsors a Discovery Day. It might be called by another name—Decision Day, Information Day, etc. This is your chance to visit the franchisor's headquarters, meet company representatives, possibly even franchisees, and learn more about the franchise opportunity by listening to a variety of presentations and asking questions. The franchisor may also include a tour of the headquarters to show you the training center, the marketing department, franchise support, etc.

Franchisors do not charge a fee for Discovery Days, but it's likely you'll be expected to provide your own transportation and lodging. If you're married, the franchisor may want your spouse to attend, too.

Don't hesitate to ask the franchisor to pay for your expenses, or to share your expenses. Depending on how eager the franchisor is to sell a franchise, you may get a free trip. But even if you have to shell out some money for this experience, it's worth it. What's several hundred dollars when you're investing several thousand if not hundreds of thousands?

Questions you should ask:

- How is this business unique and amazing?
- How does this business compare to similar franchises?
- What's the future for this industry, and this franchise in particular?

12.) Get Disclosed

Ask the franchisor for the Franchise Disclosure Document (FDD) and prepare to read it thoroughly—a couple of times. This document is written in clear English so it's fairly easy to comprehend. However, you'll probably want a franchise attorney to review the document with you.

Once the franchisor knows that you're a "serious" candidate to buy a franchise, by law the franchisor must "disclose" you before continuing to talk to you about the franchise opportunity. This is a very serious matter and franchisors are careful not to violate it.

Disclosure does not obligate you in any way! It's a formality that must occur before you can buy a franchise. In fact, until you're disclosed, you cannot legally pay the franchisor any money. The franchisor must disclose you at least 14 days prior to you buying the franchise.

Just remember: You're not obligated until you sign the franchise agreement. The FDD is one document; the franchise agreement another. However, the franchise agreement mirrors the FDD.

Questions you should ask:

- How long has this franchise been in business; who owns it; how are the franchise company's executives qualified to be in their positions?
- How much training and support will I receive? Does it cost extra money?
- How often (if ever) have franchisees sued the franchisor, and why?

13.) Go to Work for a Franchisee

One of the most important steps you can take before buying a franchise is to talk to existing franchisees. Call them, visit them, and spend time with them. The FDD includes a list of existing and former franchisees—use that list; it's one of the most important tools for franchise exploration.

Existing franchisees will talk to you by phone, or if they're in close proximity to you, they may invite you for a personal meeting. Some franchisees may not be willing to talk to you at all, but most franchisees remember what it was like when they were exploring franchise opportunities and they're willing to help you because someone once helped them. Franchisees also realize that it's important for their franchise networks to expand—it gives them greater visibility in the marketplace (more franchisees means more money in the national advertising fund), and greater clout when negotiating with suppliers.

Here's an idea that you will find extremely helpful: Go to work for an existing franchisee. Offer to work weekends, or part time, for a month or more to experience the franchise operation. This is a practical way for you to discover your interest in a specific business. Many franchisors will require that you at least meet with an existing franchisee to discuss your prospects for joining the franchise network.

"Are franchisees getting paid to tell me good things so that I'll buy the franchise?" If they are, the information will be revealed in the FDD, or the franchisor is violating federal laws in the U.S. Generally, franchisors do not pay franchisees for speaking to prospective franchisees. However, franchisors sometimes sponsor competitions, i.e., the franchisee who helps sell the most franchises in a year receives $10,000! But that information also must be disclosed in the FDD.

Questions you should ask:

- Would you buy this same franchise again?
- What are the franchisor's greatest strengths…weaknesses?
- How much money can I expect to earn after a year as a franchisee? After three years?

14.) Decide if You Can Afford the Investment

Study Item 7 of the franchisor's FDD to understand your financial commitment when you buy this franchise. Federal law requires U.S. franchisors to clearly disclose financial information in the FDD. Item 7, Estimated Initial Investment, presents each financial commitment in a chart that shows you when the money is due to be paid, to whom it must be paid (i.e., the franchisor, a media company, a landlord, or a supplier), and whether or not the money is refundable. This is the best way to see the required financial commitment at a glance.

Keep in mind that the franchisor must include every financial requirement in Item 7, which eliminates surprises. "Oh, we didn't tell you that you must pay $5,000 for training?" That sort of thing shouldn't happen anymore in franchising.

Questions you should ask:

- Can I afford to invest this amount of money?
- Do existing franchisees say that the investment is reasonable?
- How does this financial commitment compare to investments in competitive opportunities?

15.) Understand the Ongoing Fees

Look at the ongoing royalty and advertising fee requirements, which are not part of Item 7. Most franchisors require franchisees to pay a percentage of gross sales as a royalty every month—the percentage may be as low as 5 percent and as high as 12 percent, and varies from company to company. The advertising fee is also a percentage of gross sales and may be in the range of 1 percent to 3 percent paid monthly.

Questions you should ask:

- Do the royalty and advertising fees seem reasonable?
- How does the franchisor spend the royalty dollars paid by franchisees?
- Is the national advertising fund effective for boosting retail sales?

16.) Get Help!

Consult with your professional advisers. You should spend the money to engage a franchise attorney and an accountant prior to signing a franchise agreement. There are many franchise attorneys at work in the U.S. and other countries; you can find them through a franchise association such as the International Franchise Association (www.franchise.org). You will likely pay $500 to $1,500 for the attorney's basic services, paying more to an attorney who does not specialize in franchise law—that's like asking your franchise attorney to handle a personal injury suit. If an attorney suggests he/she negotiate with the franchisor on your behalf, be very careful. Franchisors rarely negotiate and franchise attorneys know that. However, franchise attorneys also know areas in which a franchisor is likely to negotiate and may be helpful in that regard.

It's more difficult to find an accountant who is familiar with franchising and who understands franchising. Too often accountants are anti-franchising and they advise their clients to start businesses independently rather than to join a franchise network and pay fees. That's unfortunate because statistics demonstrate that in many industries franchises are more successful than independently owned businesses.

My best advice for finding a "franchise friendly" accountant is to find an accountant who is also a franchisee! In other words, the accountant's practice is part of a franchise network. Again, you can find these businesses through franchise associations or by asking franchisors and franchisees for referrals. A good accountant will be able to help you develop a business plan and assess your financial risk, as well as rewards. Accounting fees vary widely, but for basic services expect to pay $500 to $1,500. Keep in mind that you also may need an accountant after you become a franchisee to prepare your quarterly and annual statements.

Note that professional advisers are not supposed to make decisions for you. "Should I buy this franchise?" is a question that a good adviser will not answer. Advisers will point out the pros and cons; ultimately, you make the decisions.

Other possible advisers include franchise brokers and coaches. When you engage these advisers, make certain that you understand what's in it for them. Brokers sell franchises for a living; they do not advise franchise prospects except as part of their mission to sell a franchise. Brokers generally do not charge fees to their clients because the franchisor pays them when they sell a franchise. There's nothing wrong with this arrangement, by the way, and franchisors who rely on brokers must reveal this information in the FDD.

Questions you should ask:

- How does this franchise opportunity compare to others you've reviewed?
- What are the problem areas that you see investing in this type of franchise?
- Based on my financial situation, is this a franchise I can afford?

17.) Make Your Final Decision

Take a deep breath, offer up any final prayers, and say "yes" to the franchisor of your choice. Go ahead; sign the franchise agreement. Congratulations, you're a franchisee! If you did your homework, and followed the recommendations offered to you in this book, you're on your way to stardom!

Questions you should ask:

- When does my training session begin?
- What three things must I be sure to do to succeed in this business
- What three things must I be sure not to do to succeed in this business?

When I'm buying a franchise, and when I coach my clients who are buying franchises, I use these 17 steps to success. Each step includes multiple tasks, and it's important to take the time to complete each step. If you have questions about how to complete these steps, or you need additional guidance, visit my website: HowtoBuyaFranchise.com and contact me.

How to Investigate Before You Invest in a Franchise

Adapted from <u>Taking the Fear Out of Franchising</u> published in 2017.

For as long as I can remember, the International Franchise Association (IFA) has advised consumers to *investigate before investing* in a franchise. It's great advice, responsible advice, and yet it's often ignored.

Too often, people invest in a franchise only to find out in a matter of months that they don't like the business or they can't succeed at the business or they don't want to operate the business, or any number of other *cant's* and *don'ts*.

"I didn't realize I'd have to spend so much time in the business" . . . "I can't handle all the turnover. I don't like working with young people. They don't want to work hard." . . . "I can't pay the royalty *and* make enough for myself." . . . "I really don't like my franchisor." . . . "I don't want to give up so much control to the franchisor."

These are among the most common complaints that I hear from people who buy franchises and then decide it was a poor decision.

"So what now?" I ask them. Of course, they come to me hoping that I'll have a solution for them and I do, but they won't like it.

It's too late to ask them, "Did you investigate before you invested?" They'll say, "Yes, of course," but upon further questioning they'll begin to realize they didn't do enough investigating. They didn't ask the pertinent questions. They didn't take the time to experience the franchise before investing in it. It makes no sense—*ever*—to invest hundreds of thousands of dollars in a business—or for that matter, as little as $10,000—and not do the necessary homework.

Maybe it's the word *necessary*. Some people apparently don't think franchise pre-investment homework is necessary, so they don't do it, or they don't do enough of it, or they don't know how to do it. And it's foolish to expect franchisors to insist on prospects doing the necessary homework. Yes, some franchisors do insist on it, but many, especially if they're eager to make a sale, don't. The law doesn't say they have to. After all, if you're in a position to buy a business, shouldn't you know that it's necessary to investigate thoroughly?

Some people will say they thought the franchise disclosure process protected them and so it wasn't necessary to give the franchise opportunity more than a cursory look. Others will say they thought it was enough to sit with their attorney to understand the franchise requirements and a "deep dive" into the nitty gritty of the business wasn't necessary.

But it is necessary! And yes, the disclosure process does indeed protect you, but mostly it protects you by requiring franchisors to provide pertinent information about the business. It can't do more than that. But *you* can. You can use the information the franchisor must provide to find out if you're a good fit for a specific business. That's where many people fail themselves. People who are actually a good fit for franchising often end up buying the wrong franchise! They buy a retail concept when they're a better fit for a service business, or they choose a food franchise but should have bought a business they could operate from home. And so on.

Unfortunately, when you don't do the necessary homework and you buy a franchise that's not a good fit, there's really not much you can do but sell the business and take your losses. It's not a popular solution, but do you have a better one? You can always try to change your mind about the franchisor, your employees, your customers, your location, your commitment, or with the hope of changing your mind about the business, but that's probably not a realistic solution. If you and the business are not a fit, it's not going to work. Get out of it. Better yet, don't ever put yourself in that position.

The IFA's advice: *Investigate before you invest* is the best way to protect yourself. Do it!

To help you, I've provided the following guidelines. Use these steps to complete the necessary homework, or the due diligence, that will lead you to make a good decision when you invest in a franchise.

Pay Attention to the Only Data That Matters

Due diligence is the process by which you "investigate" the franchise opportunity or opportunities that most interest you.

Unfortunately, many people fail Due Diligence 101. They either ignore it, they don't know how to collect the data, or they don't know how to analyze the data to arrive at reasonable conclusions.

You can do your own investigation, or you can hire someone to help you, although I don't recommend the latter because ultimately the decision to "buy" or "not to buy" a franchise rests with you.

Do you really want to invest your life savings in a business that someone else told you to buy?

Or not to buy?

Every year, even though it's been more than half a century, I still hear people say they're kicking themselves for not buying a McDonald's franchise when they had the opportunity. "If only I hadn't listened to my neighbor."

No Need to Investigate Franchising

Many experts, including consultants and advisers whom you might engage, formally or informally, will tell you that step one of your due diligence must be an investigation of franchising as a concept, or as an industry.

But I am telling you that's a waste of your time.

And here's why.

It's a Squishy Industry

No one knows for certain how many franchisor companies exist in America, or anywhere in the world, because franchisors are not required to register or to declare themselves as franchisors. Yes, every franchisor in the United States must file a disclosure document before selling a franchise, but no one's counting.

And you can be sure there are some businesses that sell franchises without filing a disclosure document, either on purpose or for lack of knowledge. These businesses may say they're selling "business opportunities," not franchises, but what they're actually doing is skirting onerous and costly franchise regulations, most likely to the detriment of the people who buy from them.

But since no one keeps track of the number of franchisor companies, the best guestimates say there are some three thousand to four thousand franchisors in North America. The number expands annually. The IFA says that new franchisor companies increase by about ten percent every year. Of course, since no one officially tracks franchise companies, no one knows how many franchisor companies fail or close their doors each year.

Are you getting the idea that franchising is a squishy industry?

Some specific data about franchises overall does exist. For example, the IFA reports that nearly three-fourths (73 percent) of franchisors support fewer than one hundred franchise outlets. Only 5 percent support five hundred or more units, and 7 percent are still looking for their first franchisee.

Many people find those numbers surprising, if not shocking. Most franchise companies never grow larger than one hundred units!

We also know that franchising as a methodology is used by businesses in seventy-five major industries, including quick-service restaurants (the largest sector), automotive repair, senior care, home services, construction, entertainment, financial services, etc. Some of the largest franchise companies are in the food and beverage industry, but some of the most successful franchise companies are in real estate, education, and business services, to name a few.

Get the Relevant Facts

Overall, franchising is best described as diverse. So how can anyone study the industry and report *relevant* data about success and failure to a prospective buyer? It's very difficult if not impossible to do. Even at their best, averages and national trends are interesting to read, but no one should use them to make a buying decision about a franchise.

If I told you that "most" franchises survive—a true statement—does that help you? There would still be "some" franchises that fail. You might think the odds are in your favor, and so while you're still a bit uncertain, you go ahead and invest your life savings in a franchise opportunity.

And two years later you're out of money and forced into bankruptcy. You can't understand it because, after all, "most" franchises survive.

Yes, they do, but you selected one that didn't. Assuming that you did everything right as a franchisee, it was just your "bad luck" that you selected the wrong franchise!

Or was it?

You can wrestle with the national data that the media report from time to time about franchising, or you can simply ignore it. Wise investors ignore it because it does not matter!

You Must Get this Part Right

But here's what you must not ignore: the success and/or failure history of the specific franchise brand you intend to buy!

That's a critical component of your due diligence. In fact, if you get this part right, you'll know whether or not you should buy a specific franchise opportunity, and you'll be confident about your decision.

Here's the good news: While it's unlikely that you can get specific data or scientific evidence, you can still determine the success or failure history of specific franchise opportunities. More than anything else you do, uncovering this information about specific franchise opportunities will take away your fear of franchising.

Once you get a franchisor's disclosure document, you can go to work to figure out the success versus failure history of that brand, and that's *relevant* data. It doesn't matter how *all* franchises perform across the board or within their industries. What matters is the performance of the *one* franchise opportunity that you hope to buy!

You may have to dig deep into a half dozen opportunities before you discover the right one to buy, based on the success-versus-failure history. But if you want to give yourself the best opportunity to succeed in franchising, there's no substitute for the work that needs to be done.

What Franchise Attorneys Say

Hoping to find a shortcut to this critical information—success versus failure—and to uncover a scientific methodology for capturing the data, I interviewed two seasoned franchise attorneys who frequently help clients perform due diligence on franchise opportunities.

Warren Lee Lewis is chair of the Franchise & Licensing Practice at Akerman LLP in Washington, D.C. He is also a member of the North American Securities Administrators Association (NASAA) Franchise Project Group's Industry Advisory Committee. NASAA is responsible for facilitating compliance with franchise disclosure requirements under state franchise investment laws.

Cheryl L. Mullin spearheads Mullin Law, PC in Richardson, Texas, a Dallas suburb, and was recognized in Best Lawyers in America®, Franchise Law, 2007-2017, and named to Texas Super Lawyers®, Franchise and Distribution Law, 2011-2016.

Both attorneys agreed that while there's no scientific methodology for determining the success-versus-failure rate of a franchise company—at least not without the cooperation of the franchisor and its franchisees and an independent auditor to examine the data provided—prospective franchisees can still take several specific steps to get a handle on a franchise brand's success-versus-failure history.

Grab the Disclosure Document

The first step is to get a copy of the franchisor's current disclosure document, which includes twenty-three items of information to help you decide if this is the right franchise opportunity for you. While an attorney most likely prepared the disclosure document for the franchisor, don't worry. The document must be written in simple English. If you can read and understand this book, you can read and understand most of a disclosure document's content.

Federal law requires franchisors to provide an annually updated disclosure document to prospective franchisees prior to selling a franchise in the United States. Franchisors are not required to give a disclosure document to foreign investors, but many will do so simply because the disclosure document is the best way to explain a franchise opportunity.

A legitimate franchisor selling a franchise in the United States will not ask you to sign any binding documents or pay any money until you've had the disclosure document in your possession for a minimum of 14 days. You and your advisers, which may include an attorney, an accountant, and a franchise or business consultant, should use the contents of the disclosure document to help you form opinions and conclusions relative to the franchise opportunity.

Turn First to the Financial Statements

Lewis and Mullin both almost immediately turn to the franchisor's financial statements, Item 21, to get an advance idea of the franchisor's performance.

"I want to see whether revenues and profits are growing or declining," explains Mullin.

"I look at profit and loss," says Lewis, "to determine if it's really a company. And if it is a company, and it's making money, what's it doing with the money? Are they taking every dollar out of the business, or are they using the money to reinvest in the franchise system?"

Both attorneys pointed out that they carefully read the notes that pertain to the financial statements. "Sometimes there is good information in the notes," says Mullin. "For example, I just read a disclosure document where the franchisor said in Item 1 that it had no predecessors or affiliates in a similar business, but the notes to the financial statements talked about how the franchisor was a successor to some other company that was engaged in the same business."

For most of us, especially if we're not lawyers, it may seem tedious to read the notes at the end of a financial statement, but a good lawyer isn't going to gloss over any of the data in a disclosure document.

Charting a Franchisor's Performance

After examining Item 21, Item 20 (Outlets and Franchisee Information), also provides early indicators of a franchisor's value, and both attorneys say it's important to pay attention to this section. The data in Item 20 is fodder for helping you determine the success-versus-failure rate of the franchise brand. However, studying the information will take time, especially if you're new to franchise due diligence, and you may want to engage one or more of your advisers to help you make sense of the information.

There are five charts in Item 20 and each (with one exception), covers a three-year period

(1) System-Wide Outlet Summary—shows the number of outlets owned by franchisees and by the company (many franchisors do not own any outlets);

(2) Transfers of Outlets to New Owners—shows the exchange of ownership that occurs when a franchisee sells to a new franchisee;

(3) Status of Franchise Outlets—shows the number of outlets opened, terminated, non-renewed, reacquired by the franchisor, and ceased operations;

(4) Status of Company-Owned Outlets (if any); and,

(5) Projected New Franchised Outlets—shows the franchisor's growth projections by state.

Perhaps you quickly realized that Charts 2 and 3 are important indicators of a franchise brand's success-versus-failure rate. If the number of transfers is rapidly increasing, you'd want to know why. Is it because franchisees are failing? Not making enough money? Or are they unhappy with the franchisor?

If more franchise units are terminated than sold, or they're not renewed, or the franchisor is acquiring a large percentage of units every year, something's wrong with that franchise. These are all red flags that should prompt you to ask the franchisor for more information.

"You cannot use the data in these charts to get a percentage of success or failure," says Lewis, "but the charts reveal a snapshot of the franchise company. The data tells you if the system is growing or if there's been a lot of turnover of units, or if units are being terminated. In all cases, it's important to ask why. A lot of turnover may be occurring because the franchisees are not making money!"

Is There an Earning's Claim?

Item 19, Financial Performance Representations, is also an early indicator of success or failure, but only if the information is provided by the franchisor. This is the one optional item in the disclosure document. While franchisors are obligated to provide all other information required by the disclosure document, they do not have to file what's commonly called an "earning's claim." However, if they decide not to provide this information, they are prohibited from discussing earnings with a prospective franchisee.

Some franchisors, in fact, prefer not to discuss earnings, especially if they're unimpressive. So when you ask, "If I buy your franchise, how much money will I earn?" it's easier and safer for the franchisor to say, "I'm not permitted to disclose that information."

You might even hear a franchisor claim, "The law doesn't allow us to disclose earnings information," but that's not true. The law encourages franchisors to disclose earnings in Item 19 but does not force them to do so. Of course, critics of franchising think that's a bad idea, and franchisors should be forced to include financial performance representations, but at the moment, that's not the law.

"Most of the disclosure documents that I review disclose financial performance," explains Mullin. It's important to note "some are more detailed than others," she says. For example, some disclose only gross sales numbers, which is permitted by law.

But in that case, Lewis adds, where the franchisor discloses the top-line revenue produced by a franchisee but doesn't include the franchisee's costs, you don't know if the franchisee earns a profit. While it's not unusual for new businesses to operate in the red for a period of time, if the business doesn't eventually break even and begin to operate in the black, it's most likely going to fail.

Disclosure Items 19 (if it's included), 20, and 21 are indicators of the franchise brand's success-versus-failure history, and the information offered in these items will lead you to the next step in your franchise brand due diligence.

Here's the Gold Mine

In addition to the five charts, Item 20 includes contact information for current and former franchisees. *Voila!* This is your gold mine. If you'll work the gold mine, that's where you'll get the answers to all your questions, including, "Am I a good fit for this business?"

The Franchise Rule requires franchisors to provide contact information for their current franchisees. In addition, franchisors are required to provide contact information for every franchisee whose outlet was terminated, canceled, or not renewed, or the franchisee otherwise voluntarily or involuntarily ceased to do business under the franchise agreement during the most recently completed fiscal year.

These lists of current and former franchisees provide a neat database for you to continue exploring the success-versus-failure history of the franchise brand. All you've got to do is contact the franchisees and ask the appropriate questions!

In my best-selling book, _101 Questions to Ask Before You Invest in a Franchise_, I provide a comprehensive list of questions to ask franchisees, franchisors, franchise advisers and even vendors to franchise companies. Several of those questions pertain to the success-versus-failure history of the franchise company while others pertain to the prospective franchisee's likelihood of succeeding in a given business.

Before contacting franchisees, it's a good idea to make a list of the dozen or so questions you want to ask and then make sure you ask each question of a dozen or so franchisees. If you track the answers in writing, you'll produce a document that eventually will help you make decisions with clarity. If you asked a dozen franchisees, "Given the opportunity, would you buy the same franchise all over again?" and ten of twelve said, "Absolutely," or something to that effect, it's going to be easier to know what you should do.

Don't Overlook Other Sources

While completing due diligence, it's not enough simply to interview franchisees. You can ask franchisors pertinent questions, too. For example: "What is the success rate of your franchisees?" . . . "Why would I buy your opportunity instead of your competitor's opportunity?" . . . "Where do you see this business ten years from now?" . . . "What's the profile of your most successful franchisees?"

Vendors also provide great insights about the success-versus-failure of the brands they serve. They not only may know how the franchisor performs financially, but they are likely to have pertinent information about the performance of specific franchisees to whom they sell products and/or services.

A vendor who provides cheese to a sandwich shop or pancake mix to a restaurant or cones to an ice cream parlor knows the volume of products sold by the franchisee. Vendors also know how the volume fluctuates, perhaps by seasons. They also know which franchisees pay their bills on time, which may or may not be an indicator of success or failure.

If you can locate vendors—and don't hesitate to ask the franchisor and franchisees for a vendor's contact information—don't be afraid to interview them. As much as they want to protect their customers, they also want to protect innocent people from business angst and catastrophes. Besides, they're not looking to take on new franchisee customers who aren't going to be able to pay their bills!

At a minimum, vendors can share with you pertinent information about territories, store locations, and other market factors that separate high-volume stores from low-volume stores.

Overall Best Source: Franchisees

But ultimately, some of the most valuable information you can gather about the franchise opportunity, and in particular the success-versus-failure history, will come from franchisees, current and past. That's why savvy franchise prospects use the Item 20 database to complete their due diligence.

You can expect the Item 20 information about existing franchisees to be current, but information about past franchisees is most likely out of date. Franchisors are not required to keep track of past franchisees or to update their contact information. Phone calls and emails to previous franchisees will most likely not be answered. Oftentimes, these former franchisees do not want to be found or they do not want to discuss their past relationship with a franchisor. In some cases, especially if the two parties disagreed and arrived at a settlement, in or out of court, the former franchisee is legally prevented from discussing the relationship.

Finding former franchisees and engaging them in meaningful conversation is a challenge.

However, it's easy to contact existing franchisees to get them to agree to speak with you by phone, answer your questions via email, and/or welcome a visit from you to give you time to observe their business for a day. Once you demonstrate to a franchisee that you're a serious candidate – that is, you've read the disclosure document, you qualify financially to buy the franchise, and you've attended the franchisor's Discovery Day (or plan to) – you'll find most franchisees to be helpful.

Franchisees Reserve Time for Serious Candidates

Franchisees are busy people and they don't want to spend time talking to "tire kickers" or people who are simply "dreaming" about buying a business but who have no idea of the expectations and requirements. They want to know that you've already done some homework. They're not obligated to talk to you, and they're not paid to talk to you (if they are, that information must be disclosed). Most franchisees are willing to give you their time and information because they share an *esprit de corps*. They want to be helpful. Besides, they may remember when they were in your shoes and they needed franchisees to help them.

Of course, franchisees also want to protect their brand. They want to be sure that you're not only qualified to buy a franchise, but that you're the type of person they would welcome into the franchise network.

You should expect that after talking to you or meeting you in person, the franchisees will report back to the franchisor to share their opinions, especially if they're unfavorable.

In some cases, however, where franchisees believe that another franchisee (or unit) in their territory would cut into their sales, it doesn't matter whether or not you're a good candidate. Those franchisees will campaign against you because they don't want additional competition. Ultimately, however, the franchisor is in control of deciding where and when to add franchise locations.

If you invest time getting to know franchisees, it's almost impossible not to find one or several who will take you into their confidence. They'll not only tell you the upside of buying and operating the franchise, but they'll tell you the downside, too.

Seasoned Franchisees are Most Helpful

You might discover franchisees who are members of the brand's franchise advisory council. Ask the franchisor for the names of those franchisees or ask existing franchisees to point you to them. In their role as advisers to the franchisor and representatives of the franchisees, they're usually comfortable talking about the pros and cons of the business and about the performance of specific franchisees. They're not intimidated by the franchisor—as some new franchisees may be—and if they've been franchisees for many years, they know the company's success-versus-failure history.

If past franchisee failures were the fault of under-capitalized or rogue franchisees, advisory council members are likely to tell you so. If past franchisee failures were the fault of the franchisor—perhaps selling a bad territory or encroaching on a franchisee's territory or falling short in the areas of training and support—they'll tell you that, too.

Other Pertinent Information

While I've emphasized Items 19, 20, and 21, all items in the disclosure document serve a valuable purpose and you need to study them to complete your due diligence.

For example, Items 5 through 7 address the fees you'll pay, including the upfront franchise fee, the ongoing royalty, and, if required, the advertising fund fee. This information details what it will cost you to operate the franchise. Franchise attorney Mullin says she looks at this data and compares it to the earnings potential of the franchise opportunity. "Does the initial investment make sense in light of the anticipated return on investment and the market challenges?" she asks.

Item 8 (Restrictions on Sources of Products and Services), tells you if you're free to buy from sources of your choice or if you must buy from sources owned by, or controlled by, the franchisor. You thought you'd buy the franchise and acquire materials or items for re-sale from your own family's business, or a friend's business, only to discover that's not permitted by the franchisor.

Item 16 (Restrictions on What the Franchisee May Sell), tells you exactly that, while Item 12 (Territory) addresses protected versus non-protected territories. Mullin says, "I look at territorial protections and restrictions. Can franchisees provide offsite services? Delivery and catering services? Sell on the Internet? The more freedom a franchisee has to go out and develop a territory, the more attractive" the franchise opportunity may be. But some franchisors restrict the franchisee to operate in a specific location while keeping other revenue streams for the franchisor's benefit.

Both Mullin and Lewis urge you to consider Item 3 (Litigation) and Item 4 (Bankruptcy) to determine the experience of the people who own the franchise company. "What kind of people are they?" asks Lewis.

Keep in mind that you need to go through this process for each franchise opportunity that you'd seriously consider buying, and the process may take you a couple of weeks to a couple of months to complete. It's a mistake not to complete due diligence for each brand even though if you're seriously considering three or four brands you may spend six to eight months doing little more than conducting due diligence.

Bottom line: By following the guidelines in this chapter, you can uncover the success-versus-failure history of any franchise opportunity and in doing so give yourself the pertinent information you need to make a "buy" or "not buy" decision.

And that's how you take the fear out of franchising!

Funding Your Franchise Acquisition: Where Do You Get the Money?

Two common mistakes that prospective franchisees make when they're exploring franchise opportunities are (1) ignorance of their personal financial status and capabilities; and (2) ignorance of the financial requirements to buy a franchise.

Do you know your credit score and how much cash you can invest in a franchise, or bring to the table to leverage additional funds? Do you know what banks, leasing companies, the U.S. Small Business Administration, and special funds designated for franchise lending will require of you to secure a loan?

The sooner you get on top of these issues, the better—otherwise, you may be wasting your time. You should expect franchisors, and franchise brokers, to ask you these questions even before they give you a Franchise Disclosure Document. Not to do so could mean the franchisor is wasting his or her time because you may not be able to acquire the franchise.

Good News for Borrowers

If you need to borrow money to acquire a franchise, the good news is that lenders are looking for good deals to fund. While there's still not a national lender for franchise opportunities, as existed prior to 2008, nowadays more community banks lend to franchisees, more franchisors lend to franchisees, several franchise-specific funds underwrite franchise acquisitions, and for those who have a retirement fund, the fund can be rolled into seed money to capitalize a business.

According to Robert Coleman, who publishes the Coleman Report (www.colemanreport.com), lenders view franchises as "a little bit better risk than mom-and-pop businesses," but they favor established brands and experienced franchisees. "If you've been successfully operating a unit for several years and now you need money to open another one to three units, you can get that money," says

Coleman. You can get the money to open your first unit, too, but it will take a little more scrutiny.

FRANdata, the franchise information firm based outside of Washington, D.C., reported that franchising is now growing at its fastest rate in five years, largely because prospective and existing franchisees have been able to find money.

How Do You Get a Loan Today?

So what's it going to take today to get the money you need to acquire a franchise opportunity?

Business financing expert Doug Smith of Biz Finance Solutions in Colorado (www.BizFinanceSolutions.com) explains that there are two types of funding: equity-based and debt-based.

"Using the money you have in your retirement plan, rolling it over without penalty or taxation, and using it as an injection to get a U.S. government-backed loan, is equity financing," he says, and it's an option that many franchisees use today.

"Debt-based funding requires a credit score and credit history to get a conventional bank loan or unsecured business financing, including equipment leasing, and unsecured personal loans. But if your credit score is weak, or you've filed a bankruptcy, it's the kiss of death."

Your personal financial situation, and your thoughts about financial risk, may determine how you should proceed when you seek financing.

The 401(k) Rollover

Smith's preferred franchise funding strategy is the 401(k) Rollover, and most people don't seem to know about it. Or, if they do, they've been told it's illegal or dangerous. However, this option has the blessing of the U.S. government, and here are the facts you need to know:

If you have a retirement fund and you change employers, you have three important options:

1. Leave the fund where it is…the majority of people choose this option.

2. Move the fund into a new account, such as a self-directed IRA.

3. Move the fund to your new employer's 401(k), thus consolidating your retirement savings in one fund.

Most people aren't aware of Option #3, beginning with becoming your own employer!

That is, you can become a franchisee and establish a C Corporation with stock and a 401(k). Becoming your own employer puts you in the enviable position of self-funding your own business, tax-free! You can move—or what the Internal Revenue Service refers to as rollover—your existing retirement money into your new employer's 401(k), and the cash can be used to buy and operate a franchise. It's tax-free, penalty-free (if done correctly), legal, and may be your best option for funding your business, particularly if you don't have other resources, or you can't qualify for a traditional loan.

Isn't This Controversial?

The U.S. Internal Revenue Service and the Department of Labor have established guidelines and directives for implementing a 401(k) Rollover. You can't use the rollover to dodge taxes, or to personally benefit from the money. Some years ago a financial broker was shut down for a period of time for stretching the rules, and that incident gave rise to the notion that the rollover is illegal. It's not. If you use the rollover for the right reasons—you can't use it for a scheme; it has to be used with a real business—you (or your adviser) set it up correctly and comply annually with the regulations, you should be able to avoid any objections or complications. Follow the spirit of the guidelines with appropriate intentions and you should remain in the clear.

Of course, the IRS reserves the right to change the rules, and that's why it's extremely important that you work with a credible company, or broker, that has a track record for successfully implementing and maintaining rollovers.

Two Benefits of a 401(k) Rollover

The 401(k) Rollover has made a good name for itself among franchisors, who frequently recommend the strategy to prospective franchisees. Here are two reasons why:

- If the franchise acquisition is a small investment—under $150,000—franchisors know that lenders aren't attracted to small loans. There's no money to be made processing small loans, so lenders avoid them. That makes a rollover more attractive. Rollover money can be used to pay for the franchise fee and to buy equipment. When you don't have collateral, or you're buying a business that provides a service from your home, a vehicle, or a small office, the 401(k) Rollover may be your best choice for funding your business.

- After a rollover, you can use the cash as equity to qualify for a conventional or SBA-guaranteed loan. You'll likely need a cash injection of 30 percent to secure a loan. In the past, borrowers used equity in real estate, i.e., their personal residence, to qualify for a loan. Now you can use rollover money for your cash injection.

"People who utilize a rollover are more successful in the average business," reveals Geoff Seiber, president and CEO of FranFund in Fort Worth, Texas (FranFund.com). "People who use this strategy tend to stay in business longer because they used their retirement money to fund their business and they don't have debt to service."

Can You Accept the Risks?

Used properly, the 401(k) Rollover is an aggressive way to capitalize your business. The challenge, however, is that by using it you give up the security of a retirement fund. Some people can't handle that emotionally. *Can you?* Will you feel comfortable knowing that your retirement money is now invested in your own business? If not, you probably don't want to use this funding strategy. On the other hand, people who start businesses, and plan to operate them, aren't usually looking for comfort.

In the U.S., numerous companies provide rollover services, including: Biz Finance Solutions, Guidant, FranFund, and Benetrends. Expect to spend in the range of $5,000 with one of these firms to set up your rollover. The firm will also offer to provide necessary administrative services to keep your fund in check, and that may cost you in the range of $100 monthly.

It's important to keep your rollover plan in compliance with the laws because the IRS audits these plans. "Under 2 percent of our plans are audited every year," says Seiber, "which is the norm in our industry. By not doing the administrative work properly, you're taking a bigger risk" if the IRS audits your account.

Options to the 401(k) Rollover

Unless you have a pile of cash that you intend to inject into your deal, i.e., a retirement fund that you will rollover or savings that you will bring to the table, your funding options are severely limited. It's even worse if you're a new franchisee and you want to buy a single unit—an existing franchisee with plans to expand, or a multi-unit operator, will find more options.

Look to Your Franchisor for Funding

Guys like Coleman, Smith, and Seiber are among a select corps of experts who can advise prospective franchisees when they need financing, but there's only so much they can do in a reticent financial market. If you can't take advantage of the programs they offer or recommend, your best source of funding may be your franchisor of choice. If you know that you will need money to acquire a franchise, look for franchisors who lend to franchisees. Even franchisors who don't loan money to franchisees know the lenders who will, so ask your finance-related questions early in your franchise exploration.

And don't give up! Some of the most successful franchisees today started out by investing in a low-cost franchise and expanding when they could afford to do so. Many others started out with money borrowed from family and friends. If franchising makes sense for you, you'll find a franchise company that will help you clear the lending hurdles.

Here's One More Funding Option: VetFran®

VetFran, sponsored by the International Franchise Association (IFA), helps veterans of the U.S. armed services buy franchise opportunities by providing financial assistance, training, and industry support.

VetFran was created by the late Don Dwyer Sr.—founder of The Dwyer Group, a conglomerate of franchise companies, to say "thank you" to America's veterans returning from the first Gulf War. After the Sept. 11, 2001, terrorist attacks, IFA re-launched VetFran and the program continues to this day.

Nearly six hundred franchise brands voluntarily offer financial incentives and mentoring to prospective franchisees who are veterans. Thousands of veterans have utilized VetFran.com to buy franchises. If you're a veteran, be sure to ask your franchisor of choice, "Do you support VetFran?" This may be an additional source of funding for you.

Foreign Investors:
Use Franchising to Get Your
U.S. Green Card

Franchising has recently become a fast-track opportunity for foreign investors who want to move to the United States. Thousands of foreign investors have already taken advantage of the Immigrant Investor Program administered by the U.S. Citizenship and Immigration Services (USCIS), and the number of applicants is rising dramatically in part due to favorable changes in the program, and in part due to franchising.

Known as EB-5, the program was created to stimulate the U.S. economy through job creation and capital investment by foreign investors. Essentially, a qualified foreigner invests $500,000 to $1 million directly into a business, such as a franchise, or into a regional fund that invests in businesses, and gets a green card and eventually U.S. citizenship, providing that the investment created at least ten full-time jobs for at least two years.

You Can Move Your Family to the U.S.

Foreign investors are using EB-5 to move their families to the U.S., or to send their children to the U.S. to study. A married investor, for example, gets visas for himself, his spouse, and all unmarried children under the age of 21. While the program has been slow to get off the ground—it has existed since 1990—more than $4 billion was invested in 2013 alone, and interest has spiked in part due to franchising.

Look around the U.S. and you'll find foreigners operating many franchised businesses. Of course, America exists because of industrious foreigners, and franchisors welcome them because they are enthusiastic about learning a successful operating system that they and their family members can use to change their lives for the better. However, EB-5 does not require investors to actually work in a business; after investing their money, foreign investors can live wherever they choose, start their own business, take a job, or retire!

A Means for U.S. Expansion

Any U.S. franchisor today who isn't aware of EB-5 is missing a huge opportunity for expansion. Many American franchisors are focused on international expansion—they want to sell master licenses to foreigners who will build out the franchise brand in their own countries—but EB-5 provides an opportunity to build more franchises in the U.S. with foreign capital and expertise. While many franchise companies are unaware of this opportunity, that will soon change because franchising is a small community and news travels fast.

What's the Red Tape?

Of course, as with any bureaucratic program, there are numerous requirements and regulations with EB-5, and it's not simply a matter of popping half-a-million dollars or more into a franchisor's bank account on Friday afternoon and moving the family to the U.S. during the weekend. The investor must prove his or her money came from a lawful source, and must also pass the scrutiny of U.S. immigration investigators. The U.S. is for sale, but not to criminals and terrorists.

In addition, the investment must create tangible employment: at least ten permanent, full-time jobs for two years. However, indirect or induced jobs count, and that's where franchising holds the trump card.

A Match for Franchising

Originally, most of the EB-5 money was invested into real estate projects that may or may not have created the requisite employment. But $500,000 invested into certain franchised businesses (in rural environments) or $1 million (in urban environments) can create upwards of forty jobs, including induced jobs that result from the supply chain.

Consider what happens when a franchisor sells a new franchise. There are direct jobs—created for the franchisee and others who work within the business—and indirect jobs—created in the supply chain. For example, when Xpresso Delight opens a new franchise, the business creates jobs for salespeople (who place coffee machines in offices) and support staff (who maintain the machines and build rapport with customers). But the business also creates jobs in the supply chain for people who manufacture the coffee machines, grow the coffee beans, manufacture paper products, such as cups, and so on. Plus there are jobs for payroll clerks, administrative assistants, and other support staff. USCIS takes all of those jobs into account to qualify an investor.

Multi-Unit Operators to Benefit

If an investor doesn't want to be a franchisee, he doesn't have to be. Again, franchising is perfect for this program. In many franchise networks, there are multi-unit operators, or would-be multi-unit operators, who seek expansion capital, and sometimes partners. And once again, most of these operators have never heard of EB-5, but they will (through books such as this, through media, and through their franchise networks), and they'll want to know how to find these investors.

Timing is everything, and in the case of EB-5 and franchising, now is the time. However, this program takes times—from the moment an investor learns of the program, finds an investment vehicle, i.e., a franchise opportunity, or a regional center, and completes the USCIS documentation, six months to a year may pass. But to many investors, that's a very short time and a small price to pay to gain access to life in the United States.

The USCIS website is a good place to learn more about this program.

How to Succeed with a Franchise Broker

By Jason Killough, CFE

Do you want to own a franchise but don't have the foggiest idea where to start? Wouldn't it be nice to have an expert, at no cost to you, walk you through the process? A franchise broker, or franchise consultant, may be the authority you're looking for to move you through the franchise vetting-and-purchasing process, from start to finish.

With several thousand franchises in at least 200 industries, a potential candidate wading through franchise information on the Internet is likely to get lost, if they even know where to begin. All of that guesswork and legwork is taken out of the equation when a seasoned franchise broker enters the picture.

A franchise broker serves as the go-between for potential franchisees and franchisors, who pay brokers to find a good fit for their franchises. The broker's goal to both future franchisees and franchisors is to create a win-win relationship. If the potential candidate buys a franchise, the parent company pays the broker a fee.

Brokers are charged with finding candidates who will be the most successful (i.e., top royalty generators) in their franchise networks. By doing so, this produces the pure, win-win nature of the relationship where all interests are aligned and transparent. If someone becomes a top royalty generator, it (by definition) means they are successful and, thus, everyone in the equation is happy.

So how do you find such a valuable adviser? Start by looking for a seasoned broker who has worked extensively with franchises. It helps if the broker is a Certified Franchise Executive, a designation awarded by the International Franchise Association.

The best brokers have worked in franchising for more than 20 years, they understand how franchising works, and they only agree to work on behalf of leading, high-potential franchise brands.

Experienced brokers have seen every possible scenario when it comes to finding and buying the right franchise. Brokers are an essential franchise-exploring "value-add" as they share their expertise in all aspects of buying a franchise.

Building Blocks and Rapport

Early in your relationship with a franchise broker, the broker will review your background and discuss your goals as they pertain to owning a franchise. The broker will likely want to know:

- Where you grew up, your family dynamic
- Education
- Career background
- Which industries pique your interest
- How much capital you have to invest
- What's important to you
- Where you want to own a franchise
- Why you want to own a franchise
- How soon you plan to make a decision

In other words, the broker wants to get to know you, and what's important to you. This will help the broker think about potential franchise opportunities that will meet your requirements.

Are You Right for a Franchise?

With those foundation blocks firmly in place, many franchise brokers will assess your potential as a franchisee. Some brokers will use profiling instruments and other meta-analysis profiling tools such as e-Quiz.net, DiSC, or another proprietary tool.

Profiling helps brokers determine first and foremost if buying a franchise makes sense for you, and if so, the type of franchise you should buy. If a broker doesn't assess your talents, skills, and behaviors, you might think about looking for another broker. Keep in mind, the broker's services are free to you.

With results from a profiling tool, you'll have a better idea of whether purchasing a franchise makes sense. Maybe you should keep your job, or look for a different job. Why move forward into franchising if you're more suited for another career option? Buying a franchise will likely require you to make a significant financial decision. Get all the input you can to make the best decision. For starters, make sure you're compatible with franchising.

If your personality and work habits are a good fit for franchising, a broker will then begin to narrow down the type of franchises to put on your short list. Brokers represent hundreds of different franchise opportunities, but it doesn't make sense to introduce you to food franchises, for example, or retail-based franchises if you're not suited for these types of businesses.

At this point, the broker will likely delve into:

- Where do you want your franchise to be located?
- Do you want to work from home, an office, a storefront, or in a mobile/truck-based franchise?
- Are you interested in retail or fast food, business-to-business or business-to-consumer opportunities?
- What are your concerns?
- Why will you be a good fit for a certain type of franchise?
- What do you have to offer to the franchisor?
- Why should the franchisor select you from among other candidates?
- What are your assets, liabilities, and net worth?
- Do you have sufficient liquidity for investing in a franchise

Finding a Right-fit Franchise

Once your broker has answers to this long list of questions, he or she searches for potential franchise brands (checking their available territories) that should fit your requirements. After introducing you to the franchise brands that interest you, your broker can also put you in touch with franchise attorneys, real estate contacts, potential lenders, and other valuable resources.

The broker may eventually give you a list of potential franchise opportunities and invite you to begin researching the brands. You can usually begin this process by visiting the franchisors' websites.

After you complete your initial research, the broker will ask you to evaluate the brands to indicate your preferences, if any. If you find one or more brands that really interest you, the broker will contact the companies directly on your behalf and make an introduction for you.

Spend Time Doing Due Diligence

Now it's time to get to know the franchisor and its franchisees. Your franchise broker might give you a checklist to help you begin this process, but ultimately you'll need to do your own due diligence. The broker won't do the due diligence for you, and you should reject a broker who suggests doing so. This is your investment and it must be based on your own research and investigation.

If your preliminary investigation is favorable, and the franchisor likes your background and profile, you'll be offered the Franchise Disclosure Document (FDD). It's free and does not obligate you in any way. It's the tool you need to conduct the balance of your due diligence (see the chapter titled: How to Investigate Before You Invest in a Franchise).

The FDD provides intimate details about a franchise opportunity. Working with your broker, it will be easier for you to discuss the significance with someone who knows a great deal about franchising.

If you're serious about taking the franchise leap, consider working with a qualified franchise broker.

Jason Killough, CFE, is a member of the The Entrepreneur Authority (TEA) franchise broker network (eAuth.com). He works with candidates across the U.S. and can be reached at jkillough@eAuth.com or by calling 1-800-390-FRAN.

Franchise Terms and Resources

The following lists provide information about franchising, including resources that may help you while you're pursuing a franchise opportunity. Please keep in mind that the inclusion of any resource does not imply the author's endorsement. The information in these lists is not exhaustive. If you're looking for something that you can't find in this section, please visit www.howtobuyafranchise.com and use our Contact form.

Franchise Terms

Here are some of the most common terms used in franchising.

Advertising Co-op
A participatory body of franchisees – occasionally including the franchisor – that contributes money to a common fund to pay for regional or national advertising programs.

Advertising Fee
Many franchise opportunities require franchisees to pay a monthly fee into an Advertising or Marketing Fund. The fee is generally represented as a percentage (for example, 2 percent) and is almost always calculated on the franchisee's gross sales, as opposed to net sales or profits. The Advertising Fee may also be a flat fee. The Advertising Fee is ongoing and will be collected while the franchise agreement is in effect. Advertising Fund monies are used to advertise the franchise brand, its products and/or services. This is not money to be used by the franchisor!

Ad Fund
Franchisees pay their Advertising Fees into an Ad Fund, which is used to underwrite the cost of advertising and promotions for franchisees. The franchisor, or Franchise Advisory Council, establishes the Ad Fund and oversees it on behalf of franchisees.

Ad Fund money is often used to hire advertising and marketing agencies to assist the franchise network.

Angel Investor

An individual or group of individuals who provide capital for a business start-up, usually in exchange for convertible debt or ownership equity.

Area Developer

The franchisor awards a single franchisee the right to operate more than one unit within a defined area, under a development agreement and based on an agreed-upon development schedule.

Business Valuation

The practice of valuing an existing business.

Buy-back Option

A term of the franchise agreement wherein if the franchisee goes out of business, the franchisor retains the right to buy back all assets at a pre-agreed price.

Conversion Franchising

The process by which existing independent businesses or dealers within an industry become franchisees when they assume the trade name and trade dress of the franchisor.

Disclosure

In some countries, and especially in the United States, franchisors are *required* by federal and some state laws to "disclose" individuals who are serious about acquiring a franchise. Disclosure is a process that includes providing prospective franchisees with a copy of the franchisor's Franchise Disclosure Document (FDD) and Franchise Agreement. The FDD must be delivered to a franchise candidate at least fourteen days prior to the candidate purchasing the franchise. Disclosure minimizes fraudulent sales in franchising and promotes the safety and longevity of franchising. Franchisors are required to comply with specific disclosure regulations that disseminate helpful information to prospective franchisees in advance of paying any money or signing any documents.

Disclosure Document
See Franchise Disclosure Document.

Discovery Day
An event set up by the franchisor so that potential franchisees may learn more about how to become a franchisee. Discovery day typically takes place at the franchisors HQ and is often the final step in the due diligence process. It provides the opportunity to meet the management/support teams and trainers face-to-face.

Earning's Claim
An Earning's Claim (or a Financial Performance Representation) may be included in a franchisor's Franchise Disclosure Document. An Earning's Claim documents the earnings of franchisees in the franchisor's network. *Most franchisors do not include Earning's Claims in their documents.* Those who do not are prohibited from making any oral or written statements concerning the actual or potential sales, costs, income, or profits of their franchise opportunities.

Equity Interest
Any legal ownership of the franchise business or the corporation that owns the franchise business.

Franchise
It's a license that grants an individual or an entity (i.e., a corporation) the right to use a franchisor's operating system for the purpose of marketing, selling, and distributing the franchisor's products and/or services. A franchise is a license.

Franchise Agreement

A legal document (license) signed by both the franchisor and the franchisee granting the franchisee the right to operate the franchise system for a specified period of time, in a specified format, and sometimes in a specified location. It's the legally binding document between franchisor and franchisee.

Franchise Associations

There are approximately forty trade associations throughout the world that represent the interests of franchisors and franchisees. See International Franchise Association.

Franchise Disclosure Document

Every franchisor in the United States is required to complete and maintain a Franchise Disclosure Document (FDD). The FDD, in layperson's language, describes the franchise opportunity. The items of disclosure are standard for all franchise companies. There are more than 20 items that require disclosure, including Litigation, Initial Franchise Fee, Franchisee's Obligations, Franchisor's Obligations, Territory, Restrictions On What The Franchisee May Sell, Renewal, Termination, Transfer and Dispute Resolution, List of Outlets (Franchisees), Financial Statements, and more. Prospective franchisees should read the FDD several times before investing in the franchise.

Franchisee

The individual or entity (i.e., a corporation) that's assigned the rights to a franchise by a franchisor.

Franchise Expo

Franchise companies come together under one roof to exhibit their franchise opportunities for a day or more. The public is invited to these events. Expos sometimes include educational programs.

Franchise Fee

A one-time, upfront fee required by the franchisor. It must be disclosed in the Franchise Disclosure Document.

Franchise Portal

A website that promotes franchise opportunities and may also include educational information about franchising. The best example: FranchiseExpo.com.

Franchisor

The company that grants franchises to franchisees. The franchisor controls and owns the franchise system.

International Franchise Association

IFA is the world's largest trade organization representing both franchisors and franchisees. Headquarters: Washington, D.C.

Website: www.franchise.org.

International Franchise Expo

The world's premier event among franchise expos is sponsored by the International Franchise Association. The producer of the IFE is MFVExpositions.

Website: www.ifeinfo.com.

Liquid Capital

Assets held in cash or in something that can be readily turned into cash. Also knows as "liquid assets".

Master Franchisee

A system whereby a franchisor grants to a party the right to operate franchised businesses and to grant sub-franchises to third parties, within an agreed-upon geographic area. The master franchisee typically retains a portion of the royalty as compensation for its services.

Multiunit Franchisee

A franchisee that owns and operates more than one franchised location.

Product Distribution Franchisee

A franchise where the franchisee simply sells the franchisor's products without using the franchisor's method of conducting business.

Royalty Fee

A payment by the franchisee to the franchisor. Usually represented as a percentage (as an example, 6 percent) and paid weekly or monthly. May also be a flat weekly or monthly fee. Royalties are almost always paid on the franchisee's gross sales, as opposed to net sales or profits. This is an ongoing fee that must be paid during the period of time the franchise agreement/license is in effect. The royalty fee must be disclosed in the Franchise Disclosure Document.

Site Selection

The process of choosing the location for a franchised business. Involves knowledge of demographics, traffic patterns, buying habits, market characteristics, wage/employment patterns, zoning and other land use regulations, building/health code ordinances, and real estate patterns.

Trademark

The marks, brand name and logo that identify a franchisor which is licensed to the franchisee.

Turnkey Operation

A term used to describe a franchise that is thoroughly organized, full equipped and professionally set up that the new franchisee need only "turn the key" in order to commence business.

Venture Capital

A person or group of individuals who invest in a business venture, providing capital for start-up or expansion. Venture capitalists are looking for a higher rate of return than would be given by more traditional investments.

Franchise Resources

Franchise Associations

International Franchise Association
1900 K St., NW, Suite 700
Washington, DC 20006
Phone: 202-628-8000
Website: www.franchise.org

In addition to representing franchisors and franchisees, the IFA also represents the Council of Franchise Suppliers, which includes attorneys, accountants, consultants, franchise brokers, and others who may be able to assist you in your exploration of franchising. IFA promotes numerous books and other resources about franchising and publishes *Franchising World* magazine. Free resources are included on the IFA's website.

Canadian Franchise Association
5399 Eglinton Ave. West, Suite 116
Toronto, Ontario
Canada M9C 5K6
Telephone: 416-695-2896
Email: info@cfa.ca
Website: www.cfa.ca

For a list of Franchise Associations Worldwide:

http://www.franchise.org

Franchise Expositions

MFV Expositions

Telephone: 201-226-1130

Website: www.mfvexpo.com

In addition to the International Franchise Expo, MFV Expositions produces regional franchise expos in cities such as Dallas, Los Angeles, and Chicago. MFV also produces international franchise events, including the London Franchise Expo and *Feria Internacional de Franquicias* in Mexico City.

U.S. Government Resources

U.S. Small Business Administration: http://www.sba.gov

U.S. Commerce Department International Trade Administration: www.ita.doc.gov

Books, Periodicals & Portals

7 Dirty Little Secrets of Franchising: Protect Your Franchise Investment, Amazon.com

12 Amazing Franchise Opportunities for 2015, Amazon.com

101 Questions to Ask Before You Invest in a Franchise, Amazon.com

Bond's Franchise Guide, Amazon.com

Buy 'Hot' Franchises Without Getting Burned, Amazon.com

Entrepreneur, www.entrepreneur.com, publishes the Franchise 500 every January

Franchise Handbook, www.franchisehandbook.com

FranchiseExpo.com, www.franchiseexpo.com

FranchiseGator.com, www.franchisegator.com

Franchise Opportunities Guide, www.franchise.org

Franchise Times, www.franchisetimes.com

Franchise Update, www.franchise-update.com

Franchising World, www.franchise.org

About The Author, Dr. John P. Hayes

John P. Hayes, Ph.D., began working in the franchise community in 1979 as a freelance writer. He continues to write about franchising for media worldwide, including newspapers, magazines, and books. On several occasions he has been a franchisee, and for several years he served as the President and CEO of one of America's major franchise companies, HomeVestors of America, Inc. He is one of the few people to have been a franchisee, a franchisor, and an adviser to franchisors and franchisees.

For many years, John's client list included the International Franchise Association (IFA), the International Franchise Expo (IFE), and dozens of franchise companies. For several years he toured the U.S. as part of IFA's regional training faculty, and on many occasions he has been a speaker and trainer for IFA, the IFE, and countless franchise companies. For several years starting in 1989, he traveled with the IFA's international franchise trade missions, marketing U.S. franchise opportunities in Europe, South America, the Pacific Rim, and the Far East.

John is a frequent speaker at international franchise expos, and a guest on radio and television to discuss franchise topics. He was featured in a thirty-minute television infomercial called *The Power of Franchising*. Through the years he has assisted franchisors and franchisees internationally to sell or acquire master licensing rights. For nearly thirty years, he has taught the most popular symposium at the International Franchise Expo: "The A to Zs of Buying a Franchise."

He is the co-author of *Franchising: The Inside Story* (with the late franchisor John Kinch); *You Can't Teach a Kid to Ride a Bike at a Seminar* (with the late franchisor David Sandler); *Start Small, Finish Big, 15 Lessons to Start & Operate Your Own Business*, (with the co-founder of Subway); and *Network Marketing for Dummies* (with the late Zig Ziglar).

In 2017, Palm Beach Atlantic University in West Palm Beach, Florida, created the Titus Center for Franchising and appointed John as the Titus Chair for Franchise Leadership. He teaches a franchise curriculum leading to a concentration in franchising for students of the Rinker School of Business at PBA. John formerly taught marketing and journalism at Gulf University for Science & Technology in Kuwait; he was a communications professor at Temple University where he was head of the Magazine Writing Sequence; and he taught journalism at Kent State University.

BizComPress

Do you have a story to tell that will help others improve their life, their business, or otherwise make a difference? BizCom Press can help you reach the widest audience possible. Founded by authors for authors, BizCom Press is a new kind of publishing company. Our award-winning team will help you write your book, edit it, design it, publish it, and promote it. And you keep the majority of your earnings!

Whether you already have a manuscript, or just the seed of an idea, contact us and we'll provide honest feedback based on decades of experience in book publishing. If we believe the manuscript or the idea has a market, we can develop a plan that fits your budget and you'll be on your way to becoming a published author.

For more information, contact Scott White at 214-458-5751 or Scott@BizComPress.com.